JACQUELINE HARRIS

GOING FORWARD OBEDIENT
TO THE MASTER'S CALL

LISTEN AND OBEY
VOLUME 1

WestBow Press books may be ordered through booksellers or by contacting:

WestBow Press
A Division of Thomas Nelson & Zondervan
1663 Liberty Drive
Bloomington, IN 47403
www.westbowpress.com
844-714-3454

Scripture quotations marked AMP are taken from the Amplified® Bible, Copyright © 2015 by The Lockman Foundation. Used by permission.

Scripture quotations marked KJV are taken from the King James Version.

ISBN: 978-1-6642-7883-7 (sc)
ISBN: 978-1-6642-7884-4 (e)

Library of Congress Control Number: 2022917600

Print information available on the last page.

WestBow Press rev. date: 11/09/2022

WESTBOW
PRESS®
A DIVISION OF THOMAS NELSON
& ZONDERVAN

This book was written about my son, Phillip Joel Harris, who was born April 17, 1985 to Willie Norvell Harris and me, Jacqueline Stell Harris. His father, Norvell, as we all called him, was a very straight to the point person. He was a wise man, many times with few words. He loved his family and worked very hard to provide for us. He was an only child who missed many things siblings experience, i.e. fighting, quarrelling about sharing clothes and things, the fact of just having a brother or sister to talk to and about. He often spoke to the kids about these things and wanted a big family for himself. Well, God truly granted him his desire.

There were eight children with his first wife Elizabeth, who died. I had four children with my first husband Herman, who died. A dozen children to start in this relationship and union but it was not the end.

Phillip was my fifth child. The number five is the number of grace – God's unmerited favor. He was the baby boy of seven brothers and eight sisters, a combination of two marriages. My first marriage was to Herman Stell Jr. Herman died September 4, 1982. My second marriage was to Willie Norvell Harris, who died September 28, 2000. Phillip was the oldest child of my second marriage, a special gift of God so special to our family and many others.

Phillip had many friends because of his outgoing personality but his best friend was Adrian Mostella. Adrian became my other son, because the two were together most of the time. Usually if you saw one, the other was close by. They played sports together in school, worked together after school, and stayed very busy having fun and enjoying life. There would be no one sad or down around them. These ones made everyone laugh in any situation. It could be telling jokes, just acting silly, or saying funny things. They could lift up your spirits anytime.

I give God the praise for blessing me with His angel for 24 years. Truly, he brought joy and life to everyone who knew him.

I now know we encountered an angel on assignment.

Jacqueline Harris

A NEW BEGINNING

From the beginning, I knew that God had a plan for my life, just as he has for each of us, but I did not know what it was. I became a widow at age twenty-seven when my husband, Herman Stell Jr., passed away unexpectedly. I was working as a nurse at the University of Alabama Hospital (UAB) in Birmingham. Herman and I had four children—Charla, Monica, Timothy, and Mary—who were eight years, five years, fourteen months, and six weeks old, respectively.

At first, I believed God wanted me to leave my job to raise my children. The two small babies were in diapers. I resigned my position at the hospital, and my new full-time job became mother and being actively involved in ministry at God's Church of Bessemer, Alabama. One of my responsibilities there was teaching the single women Bible study. My relationship with the Lord was so rich at this time. It was exciting to share with the other single women how to fall in love with Jesus and to become intimate with him and not seek relationships with men. I taught that God is our husband and he can fulfill our lives totally if we sell out wholly to him, which is based on what the Bible tells us in Proverbs 18:22 (AMP). "He who finds a wife finds a good thing and obtained favor of the Lord." This was the main theme of the Bible study. The man should be the one who finds the wife, not a woman looking to find a husband.

It had been two years since my husband died, and I was happy going to college. I was taking classes because I dreamed of creating a nursing agency to minister to elderly adults who did not want to go to a nursing home but wanted to stay in their own home. My vision was to provide personnel to run errands, along with home and nursing care to those in need. This would allow many to stay in their houses and fulfill the wishes of the elderly we could serve.

As part of my daily routine after classes, I would check on my grandmother-in-law at her home and minister to her needs. I would sometimes go to the store to get her groceries or run other errands for her. One day as I entered the community store in Raimund to purchase something for her, a man opened the door for me. As I went under his arms to enter, there was such a strange sensation over my entire being. This man, Norvell, was a minister and a well-respected person in the community. All I really knew about him was that he had a lot of children, raised hogs and cattle, and showed livestock at the state fairs. The store experience was real, but I did not meditate on it too much at the time.

Two days later, I received a call from Mary, my sister-in-law. She told me Norvell had asked for my phone number. He lived right across the street from my father-in-law and had asked them for my number.

It was a Monday when he called and said he wanted to meet me. I informed him he could meet me at church on Wednesday night. I did not date, and my life was very involved with my children and the ministry. This was an awkward experience for me.

Wednesday night came and we went to church. My pastor, Leonard Woods, was an overseer and guarded his flock well. He was very selective about the people who ministered there. However, that night, he asked Norvell to preach. *How strange!* After church, Norvell and I talked for a few minutes before we each went home.

By Friday evening, Norvell had called and asked if he could take me to dinner. I told him that I had four children and they had to go with me if we went anywhere. He told me he had eight children and that was fine. Therefore, we discussed the dinner date. Sunday was our next service so I told him if he came to church, we could have dinner after the afternoon fellowship. That Sunday after service at his church, the Good Samaritan Church, Norvell walked into God's Church. We were still in our worship service so he sat down in the back.

A few months before these events, I had had a strange dream about a man and me coming together to decide between two houses. I did remember in the dream that this man had many animals and both of us had houses. I had shared this dream with my pastor's wife, who told me God was preparing me for someone he was sending into my life. At that time, I could not receive this dream as truly from God but only as a distraction from the devil. Remember I had been teaching the Bible study about dating, marriage, and being in love with Jesus. I was not thinking about the possibility of dating or ever getting married again.

After the service that Sunday, we decided to eat at Quincy's. Dinner was very good. We all talked and introduced ourselves to each other. It was here that Norvell told me, "God said you are my wife. Now you need to pray about it to get your peace." I was so amazed that I could not say anything. I had only talked to this man three times, and now he told me this.

I was so shocked I did not sleep that night, the next night, or the next night. I was just praying and seeking God. The mystery to me was how this man could enter the relationship God and I had. We were so happy and close, and the fellowship was great. Now this was something I did not understand or expect.

After three days, I did get my peace and agreed to marry him. This was different. Many people disagreed with the marriage. I was twenty-nine, and Norvell was forty-nine years old. His wife,

Elizabeth, had not passed away very long ago, but I had heard God's answer, and regardless of what any man said, I had to obey God.

My church family was happy about the engagement and helped to plan for the wedding. A tailor volunteered to make the dresses, a florist wanted to do the flowers, and others came to offer their services. It was amazing how everything flowed together as the marriage day approached.

Six weeks after our first dinner date, we were married and en route to Panama City for our honeymoon. A few months later, I realized that I was pregnant. When I shared the news I was expecting with Norvell, he stated matter-of-factly that he knew it was a son and this was why God wanted us to marry.

Can you imagine that?

THE MIRACULOUS MOVE

Norvell wanted a real farm with actual farm equipment like the one he had seen in his travels showing the livestock. His animals were raised in the backyard of his home in Raimund. One night as we were reading the newspaper, we saw a farm advertised in the classified section of the *Birmingham News.* The description noted there were stalls, ponds, and equipment, just as he dreamed of having. It was about two weeks before we went to see the farm because it was eighty-three miles from Raimund, where we lived, to Attalla, Alabama.

When we got there, it was all grown up with weeds and bushes, but we looked over the land, ponds, equipment, and old farmhouse.

Even though it had been unoccupied for years, Norvell saw the potential and believed this was the answer to his prayers. Sometimes we can miss God's blessing by looking at things with the natural eyes of the flesh and not through faith. It had been twenty-five years of trusting God for this farm, but he kept the faith and knew God would do it.

This farm was very large with 132 acres with equipment set up to produce large quantities of pigs for marketing. I was shocked to see how some of these machines worked. The family had to do all the work in Raimund manually, but here there were individual stalls for the hogs to have their babies and automatic feeders.

After inquiring about the price and means of financing, we were told we could not get it by the credit agency. Norvell told me, "Man said no, but God said yes. It is ours. Just have faith."

We loaded up three vehicles with the family and drove up to the farm one Sunday afternoon. We prayed, anointed the land with oil, and praised God for the promise that this farm was ours.

While we were waiting for the loan to be approved, the land had to be cleared and fences put up to prepare for moving in the livestock. One of Norvell's childhood friends lived close to the farmland and agreed to start clearing the land, put up fences, and even paint the house. What a blessing he was. God was working in this matter.

It took six months before the credit association responded, but God approved the loan. It took that time to get the property ready. While we were waiting on the approval, the local land company handling the property had given Norvell the key to the house.

During this six-month period, Norvell said we had to stay unified in one accord so that doubt could not even penetrate our minds. Every evening, we would review what happened that day, repent, and make sure there was nothing to hinder our faith.

Favor from God can do more than having money. We must trust God. Do not even focus on the negatives.

We were told of another couple who wanted this land. They owned a feed company and could have paid the down payment of $25,000. That amount was a lot and we did not have any of it. All we had were faith and a promise.

Norvell worked on a plan, noting how many pigs and cattle he would have to market to generate the funds needed for the quarterly payments of $4,500. He had written down his vision to make this work.

As time grew closer to the time of the move, the hogs and pigs started dying, and one of the cows got out of the fence. A car struck it, and we had to get another car for this man. Things were looking bad, and the plan we developed for making the payments seemed impossible.

When we moved, our livestock was about half of what we started with. The mortgage payment was based on our original number of animals, and now it was diminished greatly.

God gave us favor with people in Etowah County and miraculously provided food for the animals and us. *Thank you, Lord, for daily provision.* Even with the supernatural blessings, things got very hard and we agreed that I needed to go back to work as a nurse to help with the finances.

It had been five years since I had worked apart from the farm. During this time, I had twin girls, Tonia and Sonia. This meant nine children at home, in addition to the work on the farm.

I worked two years at a nursing home to transition back into nursing after being on leave. I was hired at Gadsden Regional Medical Center, and this too was a miracle. There were no full-time positions open. I was hired in two part-time positions. One week, I worked on the psychiatric floor, and the next week, I worked on the seventh floor, a medical floor. This was a door I know God opened for me.

After one and a half years, a job was posted for a scrub nurse on the labor and delivery floor. This was a new position to provide a surgical team located in labor and delivery instead of transporting patients off the floor to general surgery for C-sections and tubal ligations. I was chosen for that position. *Awesome God, you continue to show yourself strong.*

He continued to show favor because we trust, obey, and are willing to move by faith. This move from Raimund of Bessemer, Alabama, to Attalla, Alabama, was a process of God getting us to a place of promise predestined for his will.

As we move through life, believe that the Lord orders our steps. When we seek his face, he will lead and guide us. Not only will we discover our purpose for being here, but also he will help us accomplish his plan for our life.

Phillip grew up as a very curious boy. He was always experimenting with things and loved following his father around the farm. On our farm, we raised hogs, chickens, rabbits, cows, goats, and turkeys. The cows and hogs were the main animals that my husband raised to sell at market. Farm life was difficult, but the children learned to work hard and do many things most children only read about. The boys would help their father with the livestock, and the girls and I had chores to do also.

When Phillip was about six years old, he began playing football in a peewee league. A neighbor down the street started the league. Johnny Kelley was so dedicated at keeping kids in the neighborhood involved in something constructive. He would pick up children from their homes and take them back after practice. This gave the boys an opportunity to play football, and the girls could be cheerleaders.

Johnny had talked with my husband while I was at work, and on Thursday, he picked Phillip up for practice with the West Etowah Warriors C Team. I always called home to check on the children from work, and when I asked what Phillip was doing, Novell told me he was at football practice. I was so shocked. I did not want him to play this sport because of the injuries some of his older brothers had suffered. My plan was to protect him from football. Maybe baseball, but football was so rough.

His first game was Saturday, and of course we all went to watch him play. He ran a touchdown in that game after only one day of practice, and I was hooked.

I felt I was keeping him from something he liked and God had gifted him to do. When he started football as a peewee player, he was very good and loved the game. Parents, do not overprotect your children. Sometimes, we are the hindrances to them using the gift God has placed in their lives. We supported Phillip in this endeavor and became very involved in football and other programs he participated in during elementary, middle, and high school.

Phillip was running to catch the ball during one of the games with the Warriors Peewee Football team. He played quarterback, running back, and lineman. He also played baseball and enjoyed being active in other sports image

Cathedral of Praise always had awesome children ministry and drama to keep the kids involved in activities at church. Phillip loved being in plays and did drama with the youth group.

Phillip was Joseph in a Christmas play at Cathedral of Praise, Gadsden, Alabama. Image

In 1999, during his first year at Etowah High School, Phillip played with a famous NFL player, Carnell Williams. That year, Etowah won the state championship in football. They won a state ring! *What an honor! And think about timing.* God's timing is perfect. We do not understand or know his ways.

The next year, Norvell had an accident on his way to dialysis and got a cerebral hemorrhage. He was in the intensive care unit for two weeks before he died. This was traumatic for Phillip and our whole family. Many of his friends began to spend a lot of time with him. One of his football coaches, Ty Harris, became a mentor and helped him a lot. He would have Phillip work with him at his house and business and taught him many skills. Phillip learned carpentry working with Ty and his father, Woodrow Harris. They were such a blessing keeping him occupied after his father's death.

This was a turning point in Phillip's life. He was sixteen years old. He worked with Ty and Woodrow for several years, and they invested lots of wisdom, time, and love into his life. Phillip was funny and loved to make people laugh. Ty told me about one time when Phillip had come by to pick up his check for the week from Ty's job. Ty told him that he did not have his checkbook. Phillip said, "I knew you would say that so I went by the house and got it for you." Ty laughed and wrote him his paycheck. Most people might have been angry, but Ty knew that Phillip would not steal from him.

I realized this was a time when he was trying to understand life and trying to fit in. Different types of friends were there, and I could see the struggle of trying to be with friends, partying, and then separating from that type of life and seeking God.

I watched and I prayed, knowing that this was only a season of process, for God's Word promised in Isaiah 54:13 (KJV), "All of thy children shall be taught of the Lord and great shall be the peace of thy children."

During these three years, Phillip was in church because that was not an option on Sundays and Wednesdays. I noticed that he was starting to stay out more with certain friends and listening to secular music as well as Christian music, which was a change.

I continued to speak the Word of God over him and told him not to forget God, to put God first in every decision. Most of all, to remember the call of God on his life. We must be persistent in our trust in God, even when it looks like everything is completely opposite to what we are believing and what the Word says. My saying is "I receive the end of my faith." We cannot just look at what we see, for we walk by faith and not by sight.

High school was filled with baseball and football, which took a lot of Phillip's time. Also, he was working with the Harris's at their farm, Laundromat, and homes.

SEARCHING FOR MEANING

In 2003, Phillip graduated from Etowah High School in the first graduating class of the newly erected high school. *This is so amazing at the timing of his birth.* After graduation, Phillip attended Gadsden State Community College for one year.

During this time, we knew Phillip had a call of God on his life, but he was involved with other things of the world. We kept praying, and that was the battle. Fighting the fight of faith. The enemy wants you to look at the now and get discouraged. John 10:10 (AMP) says, "The thief comes only in order to steal and kill and destroy. I came that they may have and enjoy life, and have it in abundance (to the full, till it overflows)." What does he want but to steal our joy, for the joy of the Lord is our strength?

Parents, as a parent, I know how we want to protect our children and keep them from everything. Many times our children are in the world and influenced by things they know are not right. We talk and tell them what is right, and it seems our words are not being heard. Do not stop; keep speaking the word.

Repeatedly we see them go out, and we wait for them to come home, praying God's shield of protection over them. This period can be long and seem like it will never end. Yes, it is not easy to see what looks like no hope, believing the Word of God when what you see is totally the opposite of what you believe. To receive the end of your faith means to only accept the results you believe.

F - forsaking
A - all
I - I
T - trust
H - him (God)

God's word is true, and everything else must line up with the truth if we believe and do not doubt.

In 2004, Phillip was working at a plant and living in the world, smoking and partying. Parents, please do not give up on your children. Keep praying and believing. Receive the end of your faith. What you see is only the temporal. Second Corinthians 4:18 (AMP) says, "Since we consider and look not to the things that are seen but to the things that are unseen; for the things that are seen are temporal (brief and fleeting), but the things that are invisible are deathless and everlasting." All temporary circumstances and conditions are subject to change. *To God is the glory!*

Once there was an accident with him driving the three younger children to church on a Wednesday night, and this happened down the street from our house. The axle broke and the car ran into a fence. Thank God, it was only within a block of our home and not on the highway. I was told that when this happens, the vehicle could not be controlled. *A miracle. No, a warning!*

Phillip was very involved in youth church at Cathedral of Praise. He was going to church regularly on Sundays and Wednesdays. One of the highlights of the youth group is Winterfest. It is a weekend in the Great Smoky Mountains of Tennessee, where literally thousands of young people come to encounter God and get closer to him. There are speakers, musical guests, and altar services for prayer time!

Winterfest 2005 was a special one, and I was a chaperone. It was an awesome time of prayer and fellowship, and God truly touched Phillip during this retreat. During the Friday night service, Phillip was praying and seeking God in a way I had never seen.

Most of the other groups were gone and our entire group of about thirty-five was patiently waiting as God dealt with Phillip. He was crying and experiencing God in a different way. It was an incredible sight. He knew God had touched him, and it definitely influenced his life.

About two weeks after this experience at Winterfest, Phillip was going to work and it had been raining. The Grand Am he was driving hydroplaned. It went across the median into a pastor's yard and struck a metal utility post. This was on a Wednesday afternoon, and the pastor was at home, studying his message for service that night. He heard the crash and went outside.

He found Phillip lying face down in the mud, away from the car and post. He told me that he really thought he was dead as he called 911. The paramedics arrived and transported him to the emergency room.

The car was totaled. His sneakers were still in the floorboard and sitting as if he had just been lifted out of them. He thought that he had climbed out, but witnesses said he was thrown out. Not a scratch, no broken bones, only a sore place on his hip from a golf ball in his pocket.

The insurance adjuster asked me if I had kissed my son because angels must have lifted him from that car. He had seen many accidents like that and stated that all of them had been fatal.

The amazing thing about this accident was the pastor had just removed concrete from the area where Phillip landed. He fell into mud, where only a few days earlier he would have landed on cement. God's timing is perfect, and what a mighty God we serve! This was a miracle, and Phillip realized this was another warning from God!

ACCEPTING THE CALL

In 2006, I noticed a change in Phillip. He was seeking God and becoming more serious about the Lord.

Phillip told me that he wanted to attend Master's Commission in Decatur, Alabama. I knew of Master's Commission because at one time our home church, Cathedral of Praise, hosted a class. Our youth pastor, Joe Bain, and several of our young adults had gone through the program. This was an incredible thing. We talked about it and knew God would work it out.

Being a widow twice and working as an LPN, there was very little extra money to help with the cost of the program. But when God calls you to do something, our part is to obey. All he wants is availability from each of us.

During the summer of 2007, Phillip traveled with the Decatur Master's Commission team to raise funds for his tuition, which is paid by sponsorship, funds raised on trips, and private individuals. A group in our church heard of his plans and helped with tuition for him and his best friend, Adrian Mostella, who was going also. *Praise the Lord! He knows all things from the beginning.* God was working it out. Phillip's tuition was paid for the first year. It was a miracle.

During that first year, they were involved in ministry at churches, camps, and Mardi Gras in Louisiana, Mexico, and many other places. The team ministered through drama, street ministry, and meeting the needs of various communities. Truly, his life was blessed and enriched through the travels and many experiences of ministry in Master's Commission.

There were host families in the Master's program who were like parents of the students while they were away from home. Phillip's first-year parents were Tim and Nita Clark. What a blessing they were to support him in their home during this time of transition.

He wanted to stay with the Decatur team for the second year. God was so working in his life. Our whole family was excited about Master's and the impact it had in the world. Another miracle happened when we were told he would be on scholarship for the second year. *What a blessing.* God is Jehovah-Jireh, and he does provide for his own, as we are obedient to his will.

Blessings also were his host parents for the second year. To God is the glory for all you are doing in my child's life. Phillip came home early from Decatur in March 2009. It appeared to be a sad time, but as I look back now, I see God was giving us family time with a changed and definitely mighty man of God. He got a job at Walmart in the Photo Lab, where he met a lot of people, some old friends, and many new ones. He was able to share with so many people and witness to them of what God had done in his life. God guides our steps even when we are not aware of how awesome his love and hand work in our lives. Even though he worked there less than six months, he was named employee of the month.

That summer, Phillip traveled with us on a family vacation to Florida. This was the first time he had gone with us, and we went to Universal Studios for a week. He and I were able to spend an entire day together at the Holy Land Experience. Looking back, it was a true setup from God to have a day for just the two of us. Our family had so much fun together, and those memories will be cherished forever.

In August 2009, Phillip told me he was thinking about going to Master's Commission in Denver, Colorado. That is a long way from Alabama so I told him to pray about it before he made the decision; I would be praying too. He consulted with his youth pastor, senior pastor, and previous Master's pastor. After praying, he said he believed this was what he was supposed to do. Knowing again he would be doing this totally by faith, he accepted the call.

The only significant thing that he owned was a 1996 red Tahoe. He was trying to sell it to get some money to go. He used his last check from Walmart to get his airplane ticket, so he was going to the Rocky Mountain Master's Commission. His future brother-in-law agreed to buy the truck and gave him $200 as a deposit so he had some money. He moved by faith and not by sight.

This was the middle of September and he was now at the New Life Worship Center in Colorado. With every text, he was so excited about being there and the ministry. He was enjoying the Word being taught in the church and the team there. He was so happy. They were very busy, and I did not get to talk with him much at all. One of the pictures he sent me was of him as a snow angel lying in the snow. How ironic that this was what happened in the accident. He shared about how beautiful the mountains and snow were in Denver.

Now we began the journey of a lifetime. The ten days of miracles.